This book belongs to:

Dear ___________________________,
(write your name)

God loves you very much. Jesus loves you very much. You are very important to Him.

Explore in this book Bible verses to help you know more about what God wants for you.

I pray that this book will be a blessing for you and your family.

The Author

I read or listen to the Bible every day because God talks to me through the Bible. It is His Word. The Bible is like food for my soul, I need it many times a day.

The Bible says: "Man shall not live by bread alone, but by every word that comes from the mouth of God."
(Matthew 4:4)

I know that if I listen to the Word of God, I will do things that are good and that God loves.

The Bible says: "I have stored up your word in my heart, that I might not sin against you." (Psalm 119:11)

Jesus said: "You are my friends if you do what I command you." (John 15:14)

I pray every day to talk to God.

The Bible says: "pray without ceasing".
(1 Thessalonians 5:17)

The Bible shows us how to pray.
Jesus said: "In this manner, therefore, pray:

Our Father in heaven,
Hallowed be Your name.
Your kingdom come.
Your will be done
On earth as it is in heaven.
Give us this day our daily bread.
And forgive us our debts,
As we forgive our debtors.
And do not lead us into temptation,
But deliver us from *evil*.
For Yours is the kingdom and the power and the glory
forever. Amen."

(Matthew 6:9 to 13 NKJV)

God is so good to me and my family that I praise Him every day.

The Bible says: "I will praise the LORD as long as I live; I will sing praises to my God while I have my being." (Psalm 146:2)

I listen to my parents because the Bible says:

"Children, obey your parents in the Lord, for this is right."
(Ephesians 6:1)

Be gentle with your little sister.
Yes, dad.

I am kind to my brothers and sisters.

And, I am kind to others because the Bible says:

"Beloved, let us love one another, for love is from God, and whoever loves has been born of God and knows God." (1 John 4:7)

"Love one another with brotherly affection. Outdo one another in showing honor." (Romans 12:10)

And also: "And as you wish that others would do to you, do so to them." (Luke 6:31)

I share what I have with those who do not have because the Word of God says:

"God loves a cheerful giver." (2 Corinthians 9:7)

And also: "Whoever has two *garments* is to share with him who has none, and whoever has food is to do likewise." (Luke 3:11)

I always say the truth even if I might get consequences because the Bible says: "Do not lie to one another". (Colossians 3:9)

Is it you who played with my phone even though I had told you not to do it?
Yes, it is me. Forgive me.

If I do not feel well or if I am in pain, I always tell an adult, but I am not scared because I know that Jesus heals.

The Bible says: "with *Jesus'* wounds we are healed." (Isaiah 53:5)

I am polite because the Bible says: "Let your speech always be gracious." (Colossians 4:6)

I am always happy because God loves me.

The Bible says: "Rejoice always".
(1 Thessalonians 5:16)

Whenever I can do it, I help my siblings and my friends not to fight.

The Bible says: "Blessed are the peacemakers, for they shall be called *children* of God." (Matthew 5:9)

I do not start fights or arguments and I don't maintain them because the Bible says: "If possible, so far as it depends on you, live peaceably with all." (Romans 12:18)

No.
Do you want
to fight?

I stay faithful to Jesus no matter what happens because I know that if I keep on following Jesus, I will live forever with Him.

The Bible says: "Be strong and courageous. Do not fear or be in dread of them, for it is the LORD your God who goes with you. He will not leave you or forsake you." (Deuteronomy 31:6)

It is also written : "Believe in the Lord Jesus, and you will be saved, you and your household." (Acts 16:31)

And, Jesus said : "Let the little children come to me and do not hinder them, for to such belongs the kingdom of heaven." (Matthew 19:14)

I forgive others when they hurt me or do mean things to me.

The Bible says: "Be kind to one another, tenderhearted, forgiving one another, as God in Christ forgave you." (Ephesians 4:32)

He broke your guitar! Do you want me to go break his? That is what he deserves.
No, don't break his guitar. I forgive him. Come on, let's go show this to the teacher.
I am angry because I have not won the music contest. So, I will break everyone's guitar.

I am not scared because God is with me. He said: "fear not, for I am with you." (Isaiah 41:10)

The Bible says that the Lord will keep me from all evil. (Psalm 121:7)

It is also written: "The Lord is my helper; I will not fear". (Hebrews 13:6)

I am not afraid to try on new things for the Bible says:
"I can do all things through *Jesus* who strengthens me."
(Philippians 4:13)

I help people around me.

The Bible says: "let us do good to everyone".
(Galatians 6:10)

May I help you with the cleaning, dad?
Yes, thanks. This is nice of you.

I always trust God and His Word in the Bible.

Jesus said : "Believe in God; believe also in me."
(John 14:1)

The Bible says that Jesus is The Word of God. "His name is called The Word of God." (Revelation 19:13 KJV)

The Bible says:

"The LORD is far from the wicked, but he hears the prayer of the righteous." (Proverbs 15:29)

"The LORD is my shepherd; I shall not want."
(Psalm 23:1)

"The LORD will keep you from all evil; he will keep your life."
(Psalm 121:7)

and

"Christ died for our sins, *he* was buried, *and he* was raised on the third day."
(1 Corinthians 15: 3 and 4)

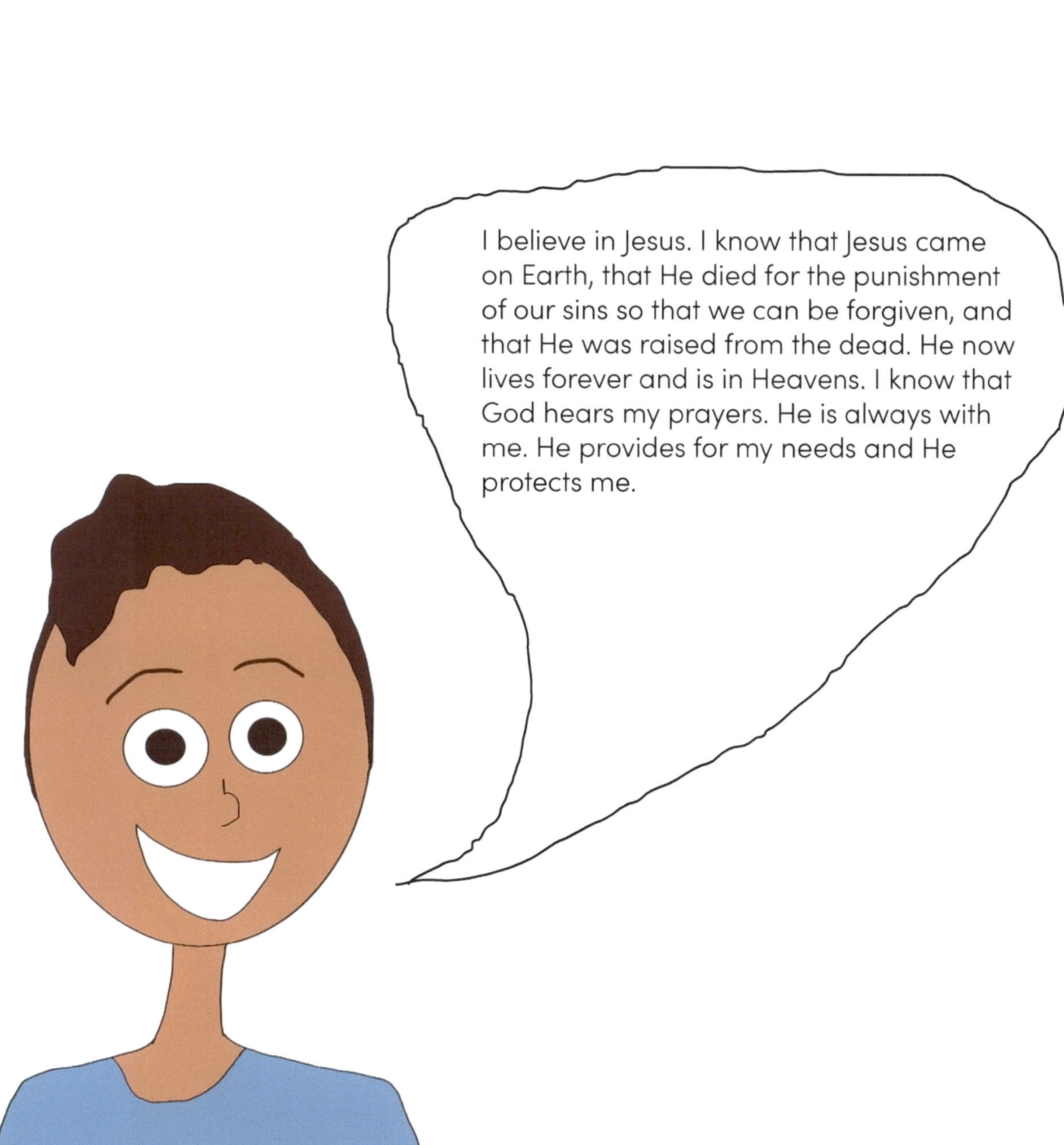

I believe in Jesus. I know that Jesus came on Earth, that He died for the punishment of our sins so that we can be forgiven, and that He was raised from the dead. He now lives forever and is in Heavens. I know that God hears my prayers. He is always with me. He provides for my needs and He protects me.

I know that Jesus will come back on Earth one day.

The Bible says:

"So Christ was once offered to bear the sins of many; and unto them that look for him shall he appear the second time without sin unto salvation." (Hebrews 9:28 KJV)

"For the Son of Man is going to come with his angels in the glory of his Father, and then he will *reward* each person according to what he has done." (Matthew 16:27)

and

"So, if they say to you, 'Look, he is in the wilderness,' do not go out. If they say, 'Look, he is in the inner rooms,' do not believe it. For as the lightning comes from the east and shines as far as the west, so will be the coming of the Son of Man."
(Matthew 24:26 and 27)

When Jesus returns, everyone will see Him at the same time. No one will have to tell me He has arrived, I will see it myself.

Notice:

The Bible version used in this book is mainly the English Standard Version (ESV) unless stated otherwise. In certain parts of the text, words were replaced to ensure comprehension of young readers. These words are put in italics.